Cardinals

and Other Songbirds

Concept and Product Development: Editorial Options, Inc.
Series Designer: Karen Donica
Book Author: Meish Goldish

For information on other World Book
products, visit us at our Web site at
http://www.worldbook.com

For information on sales to schools and libraries
in the United States, call 1-800-975-3250.

For information on sales to schools and libraries
in Canada, call 1-800-837-5365.

World Book, Inc.
233 N. Michigan Avenue
Chicago, IL 60601

Library of Congress Cataloging-in-Publication Data

Cardinals and other songbirds.
        p. cm. -- (World Book's animals of the world)
    ISBN 0-7166-1216-X -- ISBN 0-7166-1211-9 (set)
    1. Northern cardinal--Juvenile literature. 2. Songbirds--Juvenile literature.
    [1. Northern cardinal. 2. Cardinals (Birds). Songbirds.] I. World Book, Inc. II. Series.

    QL696.P2438 C27 2001
    598.8'83--dc21   2001017528

Printed in Singapore
1 2 3 4 5 6 7 8 9 05 04 03 02 01

World Book's Animals of the World

Cardinals
and Other Songbirds

How good is my grip?

World Book, Inc.
A Scott Fetzer Company
Chicago

Contents

Why wouldn't a burglar want me around?

What Is a Songbird? 6

Where in the World Do Songbirds Live? 8

How Does a Cardinal Make Its Music? 10

Why Does a Cardinal Sing? 12

Are All Cardinals Red? 14

What Happens When a Cardinal Molts? 16

What Is a Cardinal's Favorite Meal? 18

How Does a Cardinal Build a Nest? 20

When Does a Cardinal Lay Her Eggs? 22

How Do Cardinal Chicks Get Food? 24

Do Cardinals Have Any Enemies? 26

Which Songbird Can Imitate a Cardinal? 28

What Is a Warble? 30

Which Songbirds Really Don't Sing? 32

Which Songbird Can Call Its Own Name? 34

Is a Bluebird the Same As a Blue Jay? 36

Can I really sing the night away?

Whose Song Is the Most "Cheerful"?. 38

Do Nightingales Sing Only at Night?. 40

What Does a Swallow Like to Swallow?. 42

Which Songbird Is Named for an Island?. 44

How Many Songs Does the Song Sparrow Sing? 46

Are All Goldfinches Gold?. 48

How Did Chickadees Get Their Name? 50

Which Bird Gurgles When It Sings?. 52

Are All Blackbirds Black?. 54

When Is a "Lark" Not a Lark? 56

Is There Only One Kind of Oriole? 58

Are Songbirds in Danger? 60

Songbird Fun Facts. 62

Glossary 63

Index. 64

Why am I barking like a dog?

What Is a Songbird?

A songbird is a special kind of bird. A bird is an animal with feathers and wings. There are about 9,700 species, or kinds, of birds. Nearly all have voices that can produce calls. A call is usually a single sound, such as "peep" or "quack." About half of all kinds of birds can also produce a song. A song is a series of musical notes that are repeated.

Only one group of birds, the perching birds, has members that sing. These birds are named for their feet. A perching bird has three toes that point forward and one toe that points backward. The toes lock tightly so that the bird can perch, or rest, on narrow branches—even when it is asleep.

Nearly all perching birds sing. That's why these birds are also known as songbirds. A cardinal is a songbird. Canaries, robins, and bluebirds are songbirds, too. So are blue jays and sparrows.

6

Cardinal

Where in the World Do Songbirds Live?

There are about 5,000 kinds of songbirds. They live everywhere in the world, except in the far northern and far southern parts of the world. Their habitats include deserts, rain forests, farms, and cities.

Long ago, cardinals lived only in the southeastern part of the United States and in Mexico. Today, cardinals can be found almost all over the eastern, central, and southwestern United States. They also live as far south as Central America and as far north as Canada.

Scientists think that warmer weather has allowed cardinals to expand their range. Also, more and more people are putting out bird feeders. These may help cardinals make it through the rough winters in the north.

World Map

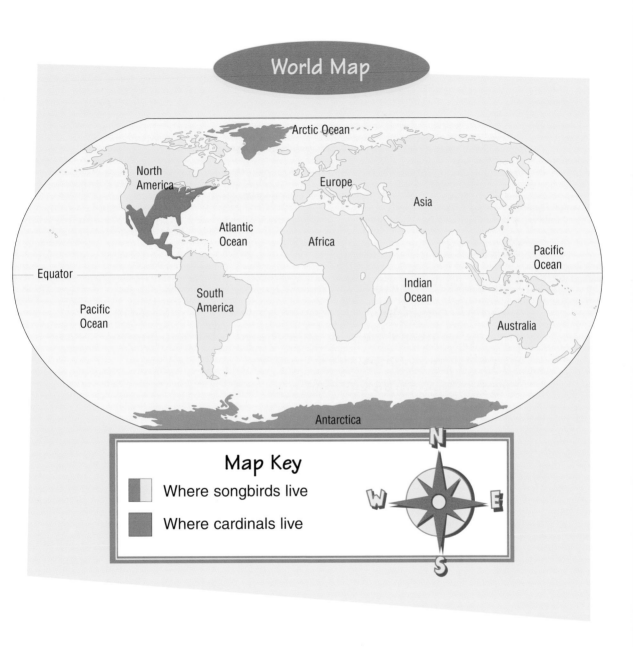

Arctic Ocean

North America

Europe

Asia

Atlantic Ocean

Africa

Pacific Ocean

Equator

South America

Indian Ocean

Pacific Ocean

Australia

Antarctica

Map Key

Where songbirds live

Where cardinals live

9

How Does a Cardinal Make Its Music?

Like all songbirds, the cardinal has a windpipe, or trachea (*TRAY kee uh*), inside its chest. At the base of the trachea is a special organ that only birds have. It is called a syrinx (*SIHR ihnks*). The cardinal uses its syrinx to produce sound and music.

Inside the syrinx are two thin membranes, or sheets. The sheets vibrate, or move back and forth rapidly, when air passes over them. As a cardinal sings, air is pushed out of its lungs and over the sheets. The vibrations create sound.

The syrinx has several muscles attached to it. As the muscles tighten and relax, different sounds are produced. A bird that can't sing has only a few muscles attached to its syrinx. But a songbird may have as many as nine pairs of muscles attached to its syrinx. These muscles allow the songbird to make different musical sounds.

Diagram of a Cardinal

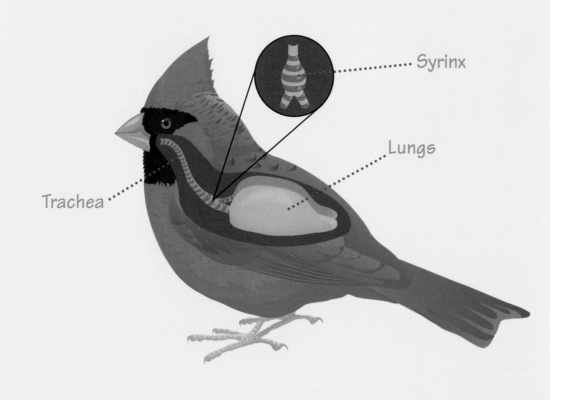

Syrinx

Lungs

Trachea

11

Why Does a Cardinal Sing?

A male cardinal sings for two main reasons. He sings as a warning to other males. His song tells them to stay out of his territory. He also sings to "advertise" that he is looking for a mate. This is why his song is called an advertising song.

With most songbirds, only the males sing. But with cardinals, the females also sing. A female cardinal often repeats the song her mate sings. A pair of cardinals may sing to each other all day long!

Each cardinal can sing about 10 different songs. Cardinals also have one call that's all their own. It's a high-pitched "Chip!" Other calls sound like "What cheer, what cheer!" and "Wheat, wheat, wheat." That's some singing!

Male cardinal

Are All Cardinals Red?

A male cardinal is bright red all over. In fact, he is the only North American red bird with a crest, or tuft of feathers, on his head. A female cardinal is mostly dull brown. But she does have a red crest, tail, and wings. Both the male and the female have black "masks" near their red-orange beaks.

The cardinals you see here are known by another name. They are northern cardinals. That's because there are other kinds of cardinals living farther south. Many of these other cardinals are not all red. Yellow cardinals, for example, live in South America. Yellow cardinals are mostly yellow in color.

One cardinal, the gray cardinal, shares areas of the southwestern United States and Mexico with the northern cardinal. Both males and females look like female northern cardinals. But gray cardinals—unlike northern cardinals—have crooked, yellow beaks.

Male and female
cardinals

What Happens When a Cardinal Molts?

Cardinals, like all other birds, molt. When a bird molts, it loses a few feathers at a time. When new feathers grow in their place, the bird loses a few more. A cardinal molts at least once a year, usually in late summer or early fall.

A cardinal needs some of its feathers for flying. When the bird molts, it sheds only a few flying feathers at a time. That way, the cardinal can keep on flying even while it is molting.

A cardinal must work hard to keep its feathers in good shape. It uses its beak to preen, or clean, each feather. A cardinal must also take baths. First, the bird dips its head into a puddle or a birdbath. Then it beats its wings to spread the water all over its body.

16

Cardinal molting

What Is a Cardinal's Favorite Meal?

As adults, cardinals mainly eat seeds, fruits, and nuts. But a cardinal's favorite food is sunflower seeds. The bird's short, strong beak is perfect for cracking the seeds open. The cardinal bites hard on the shell until it cracks apart. Then the bird eats the soft kernel inside.

In winter, cardinals often visit bird feeders filled with seeds. They also visit barnyards, where they may find corn to eat.

In summer, cardinals also eat insects and worms. They eat cotton worms and potato beetles, which may otherwise harm a farmer's crops. They also eat codling moths, which can destroy apple crops.

Cardinal eating

How Does a Cardinal Build a Nest?

In the spring, male and female cardinals pair off to mate. The female then begins to build a nest. She chooses a safe spot in a bush or on a low tree branch. Usually the nest is about 4 to 5 feet (1.2 to 1.5 meters) above the ground.

The female cardinal builds her nest with dead leaves, grass, and twigs. She weaves the material together, shaping the nest like a bowl. She lines the nest with grass or roots. Usually, she finishes the job in three to nine days. Nice work!

Female cardinal in nest

When Does a Cardinal Lay Her Eggs?

A few days after building a nest, a cardinal lays her eggs. She usually produces three to five eggs at a time. The eggs are grayish-white with brown spots and many speckles. The female sits on the eggs to keep them warm.

While the female tends the eggs, the male goes off to find food. When he finds food, the male may sing to his mate to get her attention. She then meets him away from the nest, where he feeds her. He may even bring the food right to the nest.

Cardinal eggs hatch in 12 or 13 days. At birth, all the chicks—even the males—look like their mother. Their dull brown color helps them blend in with the nest. It keeps them safe from snakes and other enemies that look for chicks to eat. When a male chick molts for the first time, it grows bright red feathers—like its father.

Cardinal eggs

How Do Cardinal Chicks Get Food?

After cardinal chicks hatch, both parents feed them. The parents give their chicks insects, such as caterpillars, beetles, cicadas, and grasshoppers.

Cardinal chicks need to be fed often. The parents bring food about four times an hour. This helps the chicks grow quickly.

By the time they are 10 days old, the cardinal chicks are ready to fly from the nest. But this requires practice! At first, the chicks are able to fly only about 15 feet (4.6 meters) at a time.

Even after young cardinals leave the nest, the father continues to feed them for a while. He also shows them how to find food on their own. Meanwhile, the mother builds a new nest to get ready for another brood, or group of young. By September, a pair of cardinals may raise up to four broods.

Cardinal chicks eating

Do Cardinals Have Any Enemies?

Like other songbirds, cardinals have many enemies. Cats, hawks, and owls hunt adult cardinals. Blue jays, wrens, and snakes try to get at cardinal eggs or chicks in the nest.

One of a cardinal's sneakiest enemies is the brown-headed cowbird. It waits for a time when the cardinals leave their nests. It steals an egg from the nest. The next day, the cowbird lays its own egg in the nest. The female cardinal sits on the egg until it hatches. Then she raises the baby cowbird as her own. What a dirty trick that is!

Cardinals have tiny enemies, too. They include fleas, lice, mites, and ticks. These pests suck blood from the birds. This can cause the birds to die. But a cardinal knows how to fight back. It picks up several ants with its beak. It rubs its feathers with the angry ants, which squirt acid. Scientists think that the acid makes some of these pests go away.

Cardinal enemy

Which Songbird Can Imitate a Cardinal?

The northern mockingbird is a songbird found in North America. Throughout the world, there are about 30 different kinds of mockingbirds. These birds are named for their ability to mock, or imitate, the songs of other birds, including cardinals.

A mockingbird does not just mock songbirds, however. It imitates other sounds as well. It can mock a dog barking, a rooster crowing, a piano playing, and even a car honking. That's some talent!

A mockingbird likes to show off its voice. In the spring, the bird may sing all night. It sings many songs and can change them several times a minute. Like the cardinal, the male mockingbird sings to claim its territory and to find a mate.

Mockingbirds, like all other songbirds, are perching birds. They like to rest on branches, chimneys, and even TV antennas.

Mockingbird

What Is a Warble?

A warble *(WOHR bul)* is a special kind of song that has many trills. Trills are vibrating, high-pitched sounds. Many songbirds sing this way. In fact, two families of birds sing this way so often that they are known as warblers.

Wood warblers live in North America and South America. These birds are only about 51/2 inches (14 centimeters) long. But they sure can sing!

The warblers you see here are yellow warblers. They are very common wood warblers. The male is bright yellow with orange streaks on his breast. The female is a dull yellow color. The male's song sounds like "Sweet, sweet, sweet. I'm so sweet!" You might think the bird is bragging!

The other family of warblers lives mainly in Europe, Asia, Africa, and Australia. These birds are known as Old World warblers. Like wood warblers, they sing high-pitched songs.

Yellow warblers

Which Songbirds Really Don't Sing?

The crow is a large songbird. But it does not have a musical voice. Instead, it makes over 20 rough calls, including "Caw, caw!" Each call has a different meaning. For example, the "assembly call" is a signal for crows to gather. Gathering together is a good way to drive off a predator.

The raven is a relative of the crow. The raven is the largest songbird. A raven can grow up to 26 inches (66 centimeters) long. That's three times longer than the cardinal! A raven's wingspan can reach 3 feet (91 centimeters) wide. Like a crow, a raven has shiny black feathers all over its body. Also, like crows, ravens don't sing. But they do make low, croaking calls.

Crows and ravens eat almost anything. They eat insects and seeds. They also enjoy frogs, mice, and snails. Crows and ravens are happy to eat garbage and dead animals, too.

Crow

Which Songbird Can Call Its Own Name?

The blue jay is another songbird that is closely related to the crow. Like the crow, the blue jay is a loud, noisy bird. It can cry its own name with the call of "Jay, jay!" Blue jays have many other calls, too. One sounds like "Queedle, queedle!" Another is "Thief, thief!"

You would probably recognize a blue jay if you saw one. It is a blue-and-white bird found in eastern and central North America. Like the cardinal, the blue jay has a crest of feathers on its head. The jay raises its crest when it's scared or excited.

Jays come in a variety of colors and shades. The Steller's jay, for example, is dark blue. It usually has a black head and crest. Other jays are brown, gray, and even green. Most of these birds also make loud calls.

Blue jay

Is a Bluebird the Same As a Blue Jay?

No, a bluebird and a blue jay are not the same. Both birds are named for their blue color. But that is where the likeness ends.

Bluebirds are smaller than blue jays. And unlike blue jays, bluebirds are timid birds. They are so timid that house sparrows and starlings often chase them from their homes and into tree holes.

Bluebirds are different from blue jays in other ways, too. Unlike blue jays, bluebirds migrate, or go south, for the winter. And bluebirds have a much sweeter, softer song than blue jays do.

There are three kinds of bluebirds. All are found in North America. The three kinds are the eastern, the western, and the mountain bluebird. Eastern and western bluebirds have orange bellies, but mountain bluebirds are almost entirely blue.

Bluebird

Whose Song Is the Most "Cheerful"?

A robin's song goes "Cheerily, cheer up, cheerily!" It is no wonder that robins have the most "cheerful" song of all!

Robins migrate south for the winter, as do bluebirds. Some robins travel over 1,000 miles (1,600 kilometers). They use rivers, mountains, and coastlines to guide them along the way. In the spring, the robins return north to raise their young.

Robins are famous for their pale blue eggs. Robins' eggs contain yellow yolks—as do the eggs of all birds. The yolk feeds the baby until the egg hatches. The chick uses a tool on the end of its beak, called an egg tooth, to break out of its shell. The egg tooth disappears soon after the chick has hatched.

Both parents share in feeding their baby robins. They give them earthworms, insects, and berries.

38

Robin

Do Nightingales Sing Only at Night?

No, nightingales sing during the day and at night. But their night singing is what makes these birds special. Most songbirds sing only during the day. Scientists think that the increase in light at sunrise is what makes the birds start to sing. When the light dims at night, their singing stops. But nightingales keep on singing—even after dark!

The nightingale is famous for its loud, sad song. But you will probably never get to hear a nightingale. Nightingales live deep in forests, where they are difficult to find. In winter, however, they do migrate to Africa from their homes in Europe and Asia.

The nightingale is a kind of songbird called a thrush. Bluebirds and robins are thrushes, too. All these birds are excellent singers.

Nightingale

What Does a Swallow Like to Swallow?

A swallow is a songbird with a big mouth. This bird's mouth is perfect for catching insects, such as mosquitoes. As a swallow flies, it opens its mouth wide and scoops up many insects—all at once. While flying, the swallow can also swoop down for a mouthful of water from a lake or a pond.

You might think that a swallow, with its big mouth, would have a loud song. But it does not. Swallows tend to twitter, or chirp, when they sing. A swallow's call sounds like "Cheat, cheat."

Barn swallows may be the most widespread of all songbirds. They live in North America, South America, Africa, Asia, and Europe. The barn swallow is known for its mud nests, which it builds in barns and other buildings.

Swallow

Which Songbird Is Named for an Island?

The canary is named for the Canary Islands, off the northwest coast of Africa. At one time, canaries lived only on these islands. Today, however, people all over the world keep canaries as pets.

Wild and pet canaries don't look the same. Wild canaries are usually green or olive in color. Pet canaries are usually bright yellow. Both kinds grow to be about 8 inches (20 centimeters) long.

Canaries are known to be fine singers. Wild canaries sing nicely, but pet canaries sing even more beautifully. The pet canaries most famous for their songs are raised in the Harz Mountains in Germany.

Canaries

How Many Songs Does the Song Sparrow Sing?

The song sparrow is a common sparrow found in North America. But this bird is no ordinary singer. A song sparrow sings about 10 different tunes. Each song usually begins by repeating the same note three times. This is followed by a trill. A whole song sounds like "Sweet, sweet, sweet, tow-bee-tri-tri-tri!"

There are about 50 kinds of sparrows in North and South America. Many of these sparrows are good singers. Among the best are vesper sparrows, fox sparrows, and white-crowned sparrows.

Other kinds of sparrows live in Africa, Asia, and Europe. One of these, the house sparrow, is now found almost everywhere. But this bird does not sing nearly so well as the American song sparrow. In fact, the house sparrow doesn't sing at all. Its call is a simple "Cheep, cheep."

Song sparrow

Are All Goldfinches Gold?

Like many other songbirds, goldfinches are named for their color. The goldfinch you see here is the American goldfinch. It is found in most parts of North America.

The male goldfinch has gold and bright yellow feathers over most of its body. The female, however, is olive-brown on top and yellowish on the bottom. In winter, the male's feathers change color, so the male looks like the female until spring.

Sometimes, the American goldfinch is called the "wild canary" by mistake. That's because of its yellow color and soft, lovely song. The bird sings as it flies up and down, making loops like a roller coaster. When it dips, it sings "Per-chik-ree!" and "Po-ta-to-chip!"

Goldfinch

How Did Chickadees Get Their Name?

Chickadees are songbirds that live in the forests of North America. This group of birds is named for the calls of two of its members: the black-capped chickadee and the Carolina chickadee. The calls of these birds sound like "Chick-a-dee-dee-dee!"

Other chickadees have similar calls. For example, the boreal *(BAWR ee uhl)* chickadee cries out "Chick-a-day-day!"

Chickadees are quite acrobatic. They like to hang upside down on tree branches and bird feeders. They eat lots of insects, catching them quickly while hanging upside down by their feet. Chickadees also use their feet to hold seeds. These birds grasp sunflower seeds between their toes and crack them open with their beaks.

Chickadee

Which Bird Gurgles When It Sings?

Wrens are songbirds that can be found in many places all over the world. In North America, the most common wren is the house wren. Its song is a long, pleasant gurgling or bubbling. The house wren is only about 5 inches (13 centimeters) long. But its song is one of the loudest of all songbirds.

House wrens are so named because they tend to nest near people's houses. They will settle in any place with a hole. House wrens have been found living in flowerpots, shoes, cars, mailboxes, holes in fences—even in the pockets of pants that hang on a clothesline!

House wrens are not the only kind of wren. Other wrens have different songs. The Carolina wren sings a cheerful "Tea kettle, tea kettle, tea kettle" all day long. The marsh wren stutters "Tip-tip-tip-trrr, tip-tip-tip-trrr."

House wren

Are All Blackbirds Black?

Most blackbirds do have some black on them. But few blackbirds are black all over. The male red-winged blackbird, for example, has red patches on his wings. The female red-winged blackbird is mostly brown with black and gray streaks.

The male red-winged blackbird spreads his wing patches over his territory. This is important, since females choose to mate with the male having the best territory. While showing off, the male sings "Konk-ka-ree!" or "O-ka-lay!"

The female blackbird also has a special call. If an enemy gets close to her nest, she cries "Chip, chip, chip, chip!" Up above, the male calls out "Check, check!" or "Tseert, tseert!" to scare away the enemy.

Male red-winged blackbird

When Is a "Lark" Not a Lark?

Larks are small songbirds that live mostly in Asia and Europe. Only one species, the horned lark, lives in North America. Horned larks share much of their habitat with other birds called meadowlarks. But meadowlarks, despite their name, are not really larks. They do, however, live in meadows.

There are two kinds of meadowlarks—the eastern and the western. They look alike, but their songs sound different. The song of the eastern meadowlark is a clear whistle of "Tee-you-tee-yerr!" The song of the western meadowlark has 7 to 10 notes. It sounds more like a lovely flute. Both songs are among the first to be heard each spring.

Unlike many other songbirds, the meadowlark builds its nest on the ground. The female lays three to seven eggs at a time. She covers the eggs with grass so that enemies will not come and steal them.

Meadowlark

Is There Only One Kind of Oriole?

No, there are many different kinds of orioles all over the world. The oriole you see here is the Baltimore oriole. It lives in North America.

In spring and summer, Baltimore orioles live in the eastern and central United States and southern Canada. Then they migrate to Mexico and South America, where they spend the winter.

Like the robin, the Baltimore oriole is famous for its bright orange breast. But the male oriole's wings and back are mostly black. The female's wings and back are mostly brown.

The female Baltimore oriole builds a deep nest. The nest is about 6 inches (15 centimeters) from top to bottom. It is shaped like a purse. It may be made from grapevine, bark strips, plant fibers, string, yarn, or hair. The nest hangs from the tip of a tree limb, safe from most enemies.

Baltimore oriole

Are Songbirds in Danger?

There are about 5,000 kinds of songbirds in the world. Few are in danger of becoming extinct, or dying out completely. However, nearly all songbirds face some dangers. Cats, falcons, and snakes hunt songbirds. Each year, millions of songbirds die from flying into windows. Many more are hit by cars.

Some songbirds have even more to worry about. In parts of Central and South America, large forests are cut down each year. This destroys the winter habitats of many migrating songbirds. Other birds, such as red-crested and yellow cardinals, are trapped and sold as pets.

Today, many songbirds are protected by laws. And many people help songbirds by hanging bird feeders and birdhouses in their yards. Such efforts are needed if we want these birds to be around to continue singing their beautiful songs.

Songbirds at
bird feeder

Songbird Fun Facts

→ The songbird that sings the most is the red-eyed vireo. It chirps more than 20,000 songs a day!

→ If bothered in its nest, a chickadee will hiss like a snake.

→ Male northern cardinals are bright red. They were named after Roman Catholic cardinals, who wear red robes.

→ Crows like to steal shiny objects such as coins—and then hide them.

→ House sparrows were introduced into the United States in the 1800's so that they would eat insect pests. In time, these birds became so common that they became pests themselves.

→ In the United States, the cardinal is the official bird for seven states—more states than any other bird.

62

Glossary

acid A chemical that has a sour taste.

beak A bird's bill that is hooked.

boreal From the northern hemisphere.

brood A family of young birds.

chick A young bird.

cowbird A small American blackbird that lays its eggs in smaller birds' nests.

crest A tuft of feathers on a bird's head.

extinct No longer existing.

feather One of the light, hollow growths that cover a bird's body.

habitat The area where an animal lives, such as grasslands or desert.

lungs Organs for breathing, found in the chest.

mate To join in a pair for breeding.

membrane A thin layer of skin or tissue.

migrate To move from one place to another at a special time to find food, to have young, or to adjust to changes in the weather.

molt To lose feathers or another body covering before getting new ones.

predator An animal that lives by hunting and killing other animals for food.

preen To clean and arrange feathers with the beak.

syrinx A special organ at the base of a bird's trachea that is used to produce sound and music.

trachea The windpipe.

trills High-pitched, vibrating sounds.

vibrate To move rapidly back and forth or up and down.

wing One of a pair of feather-covered, movable parts of a bird that is used in flying.

Index

(**Boldface** indicates a photo, map, or illustration.)

Africa, 30, 40, 42, 44, 46
Asia, 30, 40, 42, 46, 56
Australia, 30

beak, 16, 18, 26, 38, 50
blackbird, 54, **55**
blue jay, 6, 26, 34, **35,** 36
bluebird, 6, 36, **37,** 38, 40
body, 48
breast, 30, 58

call, 6, 32, 34, 42, 46, 54
Canada, 8, 58
canary, 6, 44, **45**
Canary Islands, 44
cardinal, 6, **7,** 8, 10, **11,** 12, **13,**
    14, **15,** 16, **17,** 18, **19,** 20, **21,**
    22, **23,** 24, **25,** 26, **27,** 28, 34,
    60
Central America, 8, 60
chest, 10
chickadee, 50, **51**
chicks, 22, 24, **25,** 26, 38
color, 14, 22, 26, 30, 34, 36, 44,
    48, 54, 58
cowbird, 26
crest, 14
crow, 32, **33,** 34

eating habits, 16, 18, **19,** 24, **25,**
    32, 38, 50
eggs, 22, **23,** 26, 38, 56

enemies, 26, **27,** 56, 58
Europe, 30, 40, 42, 46, 56
extinction, 60

feathers, 6, 14, 16, 22, 26, 32, 34, 48
feet, 6
flying, 16

Germany, 44
goldfinch, 48, **49**

habitat, 8, 44, 50, 60
hatch, 22, 38
head, 14, 16, 34

lark, 56
living habits, 6, 12, 20, 22, 24,
    28, 42, 52, 56
lungs, 10, **11**

mate, 12, 20, 28, 54
meadowlark, 56, **57**
Mexico, 8, 14, 58
migration, 36, 38, 40, 58
mockingbird, 28, **29**
molting, 16, **17,** 22
mouth, 42
movement, 50

nest, 20, **21,** 22, 24, 26, 42, 56,
    58
nightingale, 40, **41**
North America, 8, 28, 30, 34, 36,
    42, 46, 48, 50, 52, 54, 58

oriole, 58, **59**

perching bird, 6, 28
protection, 22, 26, 60

raven, 32
robin, 6, 38, **39,** 40, 58

sing, 6, 10, 12, 22, 28, 30, 32, 36,
    38, 40, 42, 44, 46, 48, 52, 56,
    60
size, 30, 32, 36, 44, 58
South America, 14, 30, 42, 46,
    54, 58, 60
sparrow, 6, 46, **47**
species, 6, 8, 28, 46, 60
swallow, 42, **43**
syrinx, 10, **11**

tail, 14
thrush, 40
toes, 6
trachea, 10, **11**
trill, 30, 46

United States, 8, 14, 58

warble, 30
warbler, 30, **31**
windpipe, 10
wings, 6, 14, 16, 54, 58
world map, **9**
wren, 26, 52, **53**

Picture Acknowledgments: Front & Back Cover: © Jen & Des Bartlett, Bruce Coleman Inc.; © Stephen Dalton, Photo Researchers;
© Bill Goulet, Bruce Coleman Inc.; © Steve Maslowski, Photo Researchers; © Joe McDonald, Bruce Coleman Inc.

© Jen & Des Bartlett, Bruce Coleman Inc. 3; © Robert P. Carr, Bruce Coleman Inc. 53, © Robert P. Carr, Bruce Coleman Collection 57;
© Stephen Dalton, Photo Researchers 43; © Larry Ditto, Bruce Coleman Inc. 17; © John Gerlach, Tom Stack & Associates 39;
© Bill Goulet, Bruce Coleman Inc. 5, 29; © Stephen J. Krasemann, Bruce Coleman Collection 7; © Wayne Lankinen, Bruce Coleman
Collection 37; © Steve Maslowski, Photo Researchers 15, 49; © Steve & Dave Maslowski, Photo Researchers 61; © Joe McDonald,
Bruce Coleman Inc. 33; © Anthony Mercieca, Photo Researchers 27, 31; © Scott Nielsen, Bruce Coleman Inc. 59; © Marie Read, Bruce
Coleman Collection 4, 35, 51; © Hans Reinhard, Bruce Coleman Inc. 45; © A. Rider, Photo Researchers 47; © Laura Riley, Bruce Coleman
Inc. 13, 21; © Delbert Rust, Photo Researchers 23; © Gregory K. Scott, Photo Researchers 25; © Helen Williams, Photo Researchers 19;
© Roger Wilmshurst, Photo Researchers 5, 41; © Jim Zipp, Photo Researchers 55.

Illustrations: WORLD BOOK illustration by Michael DiGiorgio 9, 13, 21, 27; WORLD BOOK illustration by Karen Donica 9, 62.

Songbird Classification

Scientists classify animals by placing them into groups. The animal kingdom is a group that contains all the world's animals. Phylum, class, order, and family are smaller groups. Each phylum contains many classes. A class contains orders, and a family contains individual species. Each species also has its own scientific name. Here is how the animals in this book fit in to this system.

Animals with backbones and their relatives (Phylum Chordata)

Birds (Class Aves)

Songbirds and other perching birds (Order Passeriformes)

American sparrows and their relatives (Family Emberizidae)

Fox sparrow . . . . *Passerella iliaca*
Red-crested cardinal . . . . *Paroaria coronata*
Song sparrow . . . . *Melospiza melodia*
Vesper sparrow . . . . *Pooecetes gramineus*
White-crowned sparrow . . . . *Zonotrichia leucophrys*
Yellow cardinal . . . . *Gubernatrix cristata*

Blackbirds and their relatives (Family Icteridae)

Baltimore oriole . . . . *Icterus galbula*
Brown-headed cowbird . . . . . *Molothrus ater*
Bullock's oriole . . . . *Icterus bullockii*
Eastern meadowlark . . . . *Sturnella magna*
Red-winged blackbird . . . . . . *Agelaius phoeniceus*
Western meadowlark . . . . *Sturnella neglecta*

Chickadees and their relatives (Family Paridae)

Black-capped chickadee . . . . . *Parus atricapilla*
Boreal chickadee . . . . *Parus hudsonica*
Carolina chickadee . . . . *Parus carolinensis*

Cardinals and their relatives (Family Cardinalidae)

Northern cardinal . . . . *Cardinalis cardinalis*
Pyrrhuloxia . . . . *Cardinalis sinuatus*
Vermillion cardinal . . . . *Cardinalis phoeniceus*

Crows, Jays, and their relatives (Family Corvidae)

Blue jay . . . . *Cyanocitta cristata*
American crow . . . . *Corvus brachyrhynchos*
Common raven . . . . *Corvus corax*
Stellar's jay . . . . *Cyanocitta stelleri*

Finches (Family Fringillidae)

American goldfinch . . . . *Carduelis tristis*
Canary . . . . *Serinus canaria*

Larks (Family Alaudidae)

Horned lark . . . . *Eremophila alpestris*

Mockingbirds and their relatives (Family Mimidae)

Northern mockingbird . . . . . . *Mimus polyglottos*

Old World sparrows and their relatives (Family Passeridae)

House sparrow . . . . *Passer domesticus*

Old World warblers and their relatives (Family Sylviidae)

Starlings and their relatives (Family Sturnidae)

Starling . . . . *Sturnus vulgaris*

Swallows (Family Hirundininae)

Barn swallow . . . . *Hirundo rustica*
Cliff swallow . . . . *Hirundo pyrrhonota*

Thrushes and their relatives (Family Turdidae)

American robin . . . . *Turdus migratorius*
Eastern bluebird . . . . *Sialia sialis*
Mountain bluebird . . . . *Sialia currucoides*
Nightingale . . . . *Luscinia megarhynchos*
Western bluebird . . . . *Sialia mexicana*

Vireos (Family Vireonidae)

Red-eyed vireo . . . . *Vireo olivaceus*

Wood warblers (Family Parulidae)

Yellow warbler . . . . *Dendroica petechia*

Wrens (Family Troglodytidae)

Carolina wren . . . . *Thryothorus ludovicianus*
House wren . . . . *Troglodytes aedon*
Marsh wren . . . . *Cistothorus palustris*